# Bloom

# Book 2

A 90-Day Devotional
By Samantha Hanni

BLOOM BOOK 2
2018 First Edition
Printed by CreateSpace
ISBN-13: 978-1717205407
ISBN-10: 1717205402

# Table of Contents

For my Maloy and Hanni families

For Leah

# Welcome!

Hi friend!

I am so glad you are going to join me on this adventure called life. Life can get pretty crazy, am I right? There are many voices demanding your attention. Voices that tell you how to look, how to dress, who to be, what to believe in. And just as you figure out the look you want or the group you want to be a part of, the rules change, and you're left once again to figure out where you fit in.

How do you know which is the right voice or the right idea? How do you know which voice to listen to? As you read through these pages, it's my hope that you will know which voice you can always trust: God's. It's my prayer that you will grow in your understanding of what it means to be a child of God, a daughter of the King. Sound good to you? Keep reading.

Maybe you're wondering why I've named this series "Bloom." Well, in nature, there is beauty in each stage of a flower blooming. From a tight bud, to unfurled petals in all their glory, there is beauty. I want you to know there is beauty in each stage of growing up. Yes, you will experience awkward and uncomfortable times during these years, but be encouraged! You are lovely in God's sight, no matter what's happened during the day. There is nothing you can do (or not do) to make you unlovely in God's sight. He loves to look down on his garden to smile at his children growing at different times and in different ways.

Here's how this book works. Each day there will be a scripture to read and a few thoughts to help you apply that scripture to your life.

In the "What About Me" section, sometimes there will be a question, prayer, or action for you to take. Sometimes, there won't be anything but a blank space, and you can use that to write whatever is on your heart and share it with God. It's your space.

My prayer is that this book becomes like a friend, accompanying you on your journey to blooming into the young woman God desires. May it encourage you to open into the lovely flower the Lord created you to be.

Are you ready to bloom?

# Part 1:
## Family Matters

# *Getting Started*

What makes up a family? If you could peek into living rooms all across the world, you would see families in all shapes, sizes, scents, and colors. Moms, dads, siblings, aunts and uncles, grandparents, godparents, foster parents, adoptive parents, and everything in between. The family is usually wonderful, but often it can have lots of moving pieces, and it's hard to know how to navigate those shifting pieces sometimes, especially as you get older. In this section, we will look at different family relationships and how God wants to relate to them. Are you ready? Grab your Bible and let's get started.

# Day 1: Family First

As God looked over the Garden of Eden at the beginning of time, he had a plan for how humans would grow and live together: through a family. God created family first. He didn't create a school, a government, a team, or a club. He chose to create a family.

---

"So God created mankind in his own image, in the image of God he created them; male and female he created them."
Genesis 1:27

---

Families are important in God's kingdom because they provide a unique network of support, teaching, and love. Marriages stretch men and women to become more like God, to learn about sacrifice, and work as a team. Through marriages, children are born and can learn about God, which in turn grows and strengthens the kingdom. Just like we said in the intro to this section, there is not one type of family. And no one family is perfect. But through it all, God wants you to know how much he loves you and has a plan for you and your family, even when you make mistakes.

## What about me?

Families come in all shapes and sizes. What does your family look like? Use the space below to write or draw your family. Next to each person's name, write one thing you can be praying about for them, or write something you are thankful for about them.

# Day 2: The Mission

When you are born, God gives your parents an important mission.

As parents, they care for your needs, love you, and teach you. If your parents are followers of Christ, their mission includes teaching you about him! They can't make decisions for you, but they are charged with sharing about God and demonstrating his character with their words and actions.

---

"These commandments that I give you today are to be on your hearts. Impress them on your children. Talk about them when you sit at home and when you walk along the road, when you lie down and when you get up. Tie them as symbols on your hands and bind them on your foreheads. Write them on the doorframes of your houses and on your gates."
Deuteronomy 6:6-9

---

Moms and dads have been given serious instructions to make the most of every opportunity they have to point the way to Christ. They are to talk about the things of God whether you all are cooking dinner, running errands, or on vacation. And every day, you have a choice whether to help your parents or hinder them as they carry out their mission. What will your choice be?

## What about me?

Will you make the choice to listen, to respond quickly, and to react with a joyful spirit? Will you choose to ask questions when you don't understand, rather than sulking or pouting? Even if your parents aren't Christians, you can still fulfill God's mission for you by doing these same things.

# Day 3: Your Biggest Fans

Grandparents come in all shapes and sizes. Some are younger grandparents, some are older. Some live close to you (maybe even with you!) and some live far away.

Maybe they died before you were born and you never got to meet them. Maybe you see them every day. Maybe they enjoy taking you on fun outings, like getting ice cream, going fishing or hunting, or coming to your recitals. Maybe they stay at home and like to do quiet things, like board games or crafts.

Whatever shape and size your grandparents are, it is important to Jesus that you show them love and respect. Grandparents are often your first friends and biggest fans. In fact, here is what the Bible has to say about that:

---

"Grandchildren are the crown of old men…"
Proverbs 17:6a (NASB)

---

Did you hear that? You are a crown, a reward for your grandparents! When we read this scripture, it's not so we can get a big head. We read it to remind ourselves how important it is to love our grandparents and spend time with them. One day our grandparents won't be here. But if we have lots of memories and stories to look back on with them, but it will make their absence a little easier.

## What about me?

How can you keep making special memories with your grandparents? List some ways in the space below.

# Day 4: In Over My Head

One day not long after I had finished the first grade, my mom took my younger brother and me to go swimming at a friend's neighborhood pool. On the way to the pool, she told me to avoid the deep end, since I couldn't swim well yet, and I couldn't reach the bottom.

Thinking I knew better, I slid into the deep end after we had been swimming a while. Water closed over my head. I had made a BIG mistake.

Two seconds later, my mom was hauling me out of the water, disaster avoided. Shivering, I realized in my moment of disobedience, I'd put myself in a dangerous situation. My mom hadn't given me that rule to keep me from having fun or to make me feel like a baby. She told me to stay out of the deep end so I could keep having fun and stay safe.

---

"Children, obey your parents in the Lord, for this is right. 'Honor your father and mother'— which is the first commandment with a promise— so that it may go well with you and that you may enjoy long life on the earth."
Ephesians 6:1-3

---

What does this scripture mean? When we obey our parents, we obey God, too. Through that obedience, God's blessings can flow.

## What about me?

Our parents know what's best for us and have our best interests at heart. The day I disobeyed my mom at the pool, I could've drowned. All because I didn't listen to her. I encourage you to choose to obey God by obeying your parents and other authorities in your lives and trust that they are looking out for you.

# Day 5: Oh, Brother!

> "Behold, how good and pleasant it is when
> brothers dwell in unity!"
> Psalm 133:1

Do you have any siblings? I have one younger brother who is three years younger than me. My husband also has one younger brother. Siblings are a wonderful gift from God because you get to share life and family memories in a special way, but I can assure you that siblings don't always "dwell in unity." Family members see each other at their best, but also at their worst. That's what makes dwelling in unity difficult.

Families also go through different seasons, and transitioning from one season to the next can be hard. When siblings are born, you move up in school, or when a sibling moves out on their own, those are all big changes for the family to process.

But those struggles and changes aren't too big for God. I would encourage you to regularly pray for your siblings, especially during a time of change, and make it your goal to treat them like the best friends they can be. You just might be surprised to gain a new friend.

## What about me?

In the space below, list out one or two things that you are grateful for about your siblings. You can also record prayers for them: for help in school, coming to know the Lord, for them to find good friends, for your relationship. Keep track of how the Lord answers those prayers in the coming months and years.

# Day 6: Role Model

Who are the role models in your life? People that you look up to and admire and want to be like? There are a handful of people in my life that I admire and I try to follow their example. Have you ever thought that you might be a role model for someone else?

Whether it's your siblings or younger kids at your church, school, dance, or another activity you participate in, I'm willing to bet there's at least one person who already looks up to you and admires you. In my circle of friends, during middle school and even high school, it wasn't considered cool to be friends with the younger girls. How silly is that! I chose to be friendly to all (even if the girls were younger than me) and I ended up with some great friends. One of those girls introduced me to my husband years later. You just never know how God will use those friendships!

Younger kids look up to you, whether you realize it or not. They're watching how you talk to your friends, how you listen to your parents, and how you do all the other things you do when you think no one else is looking. You never know how an action of yours might affect someone else, so don't underestimate your influence. Treasure the relationships you have with those who are younger than you. It just might change your life.

"Therefore, as we have opportunity, let us do
good to all people, especially to those who
belong to the family of believers."
Galatians 6:10

What about me?

What are a few things you can do this week to reach
out to someone younger than you and make them feel
special? List them in the space below.

# Day 7: Shades of Jealousy

Seems like everything is either about Baylee or Baby Macie, Tori complained to herself.

Tori is the middle of three girls. Baylee, the oldest, is amazing on the soccer field and a great student. And Baby Macie? Well, who doesn't want to hold a gurgling, smiley baby?

Tori didn't play any sports, and even though she was in Girl Scouts, she wasn't sure if she liked it anymore. She wanted someone to pay attention to her for once. No one seemed to notice quiet, good-natured Tori. At home, her parents were distracted by the needs of the baby, and most conversation seemed to revolve around how Baylee had played her last game.

Do you ever have days like Tori? Do you get jealous for your family's or friends' attention?

You're not alone. Even if you go through seasons of your life when it feels like others get more attention than you, know that at all times, God sees you, notices you, and loves you. The Bible says that not even our sighs are hidden from him! That must mean he is paying close attention to us! (Psalm 38:9)

Don't think you're getting lost in the crowd. Jesus thinks you are special and worth talking about. Jesus doesn't have any "oldest" or "middle" children. He loves each one of us and has enough attention for all of us.

# What about me?

# Day 8: Who's the Boss?

In the space below, make a list of the people who have authority in your life. Your list might include parents, grandparents, teachers, coaches, or babysitters.

I'm betting that sometimes, it's not fun when you have to stop watching your show to clean your room, walk the dog, or take out the trash. Maybe it doesn't seem fair. Maybe you just don't like doing what others tell you to do. Let's see what God's word has to say about that kind of attitude.

---

"Let everyone be subject to the governing authorities, for there is no authority except that which God has established... Consequently, whoever rebels against the authority is rebelling against what God has instituted, and those who do so will bring judgment on themselves. For rulers hold no terror for those who do right, but for those who do wrong."
Romans 13:1-3a

---

What does this mean? God says that everyone should (kids included) submit to the authorities in their lives. No one is excluded from that. This verse also tells us that it's God who has created earthly authorities and bosses, so by disobeying and disrespecting those authorities in our lives (like the ones listed below), we are disobeying God.

Finally, if we are doing what we're supposed to be doing, we shouldn't be afraid that we are going to get in trouble, like with a teacher or policeman. Their job is to take care of those who are doing right but stop those who are doing wrong. We honor God when we follow authority. No, earthly authority isn't perfect, but when we obey, we walk in God's authority and protections, which is perfect.

## What about me?

Do you have a hard time submitting to authority? Spend a few minutes telling God about your struggle, and asking him for his help.

# Day 9: A Special Companion

Today, we're going to hear from my friend Rebekah on growing up with a sibling with special needs.

---

"And even though my illness was a trial to you, you did not treat me with contempt or scorn. Instead, you welcomed me as if I were an angel of God, as if I were Christ Jesus himself." Galatians 4:14

---

*You have been given a special assignment from the Lord. Out of everyone in the world, God chose you to grow up with your special-needs brother or sister. God chose you to be a best friend, an encourager, and a companion to walk alongside your sibling on this difficult journey of disability in its various forms. It is not a coincidence or an accident that you were put into the same family. Yes, your path may be a bit steeper and more challenging at times than the paths of your friends. You will most likely experience times of loneliness, misunderstanding, and embarrassment. You may sometimes find yourself wishing for a more "normal" life.*

*However, if you stop and look from God's perspective, you will see that you also have the rare privilege of experiencing unique joys and victories that others do not. You have your very own special teacher in your sibling to teach you lessons, lessons that you can truly learn as you use each day as an opportunity to practice.*

*The Lord has sent your sibling as a cherished gift from heaven to develop in you the character traits that he knows you need to become more like Him. God will use your special sibling to teach you how to be more patient, compassionate, and humble.*

*As you stand up for your sibling in awkward or uncomfortable situations, God will develop in you a sense of justice and an awareness of others. As you watch your sibling minister to others in his or her own unique way, you will see that God's work is not limited by our human imperfections.*

*You will not always be the perfect sister. You will fail to be patient and not always feel compassion. You will say things and make choices that you'll regret later. But in those times, God forgives and gives a fresh start. God has not asked you to take on this role without fully equipping you to carry out the task. He chose you for this important job because he knows that with his help, you can rise to the occasion and live out this divine calling.*

## What about me?

# Day 10: What's in a Name?

I love learning what people's names mean. Do you know what your name means? Jot it down here if you know. If you don't know, go ask your parents!

One of the meanings for my name (Samantha) is "listener of God." One who has their ear turned toward God. As humans, it's tempting to think we know it all, that we don't need any help or counsel. To be a good listener is to be teachable, to be humble and ready to learn in any situation.

One of my favorite verses is Isaiah 50:4-5.

"The Sovereign Lord has given me a well-instructed tongue, to know the word that sustains the weary. He wakens me morning by morning, wakens my ear to listen like one being instructed. The Sovereign Lord has opened my ears; I have not been rebellious, I have not turned away."

Throughout scripture, God beckons us to open our ears, to turn toward him. And you are never too young to start listening to God. Are your ears open toward God? Or do you tend to be rebellious and turn away? Let God teach you.

## What about me?

Pray this with me:

Lord, let my ears be open toward you and have a teachable heart. Help me turn toward you and not away from you. In Jesus' name, amen.

# Day 11: Respect the Elderly

You may not realize this yet, but sometimes our culture doesn't do a good job of honoring those who are older. We get impatient with them when they don't hear us the first time, and we get irritated when they don't understand what the latest emojis mean or how to post to Instagram. We hurry them along from store to store. We don't listen with both ears when they are sharing stories from years gone by because they're slow, and TBH, sometimes the stories seem boring.

We don't always show them the respect they need. Instead, our culture focuses on younger generations. While that's not wrong, it is wrong to completely disregard other age groups.

Other cultures, like ones in Asian countries, show continued respect to the elderly throughout their life. Young people take what their elders have to say seriously, they listen to them, and they are patient with them. To be elderly is to be respected in the community in many cultures across the world.

> "Gray hair is a crown of splendor; it is attained in the way of righteousness."
> Proverbs 16:31

Throughout his time on earth, Jesus reached across all people groups: people from other cultures, men with fancy jobs, and men with un-fancy jobs, women from all walks of life, and of course, kids. He included all ages of people. His example should be our example.

## What about me?

Treat those who are older with respect and take time to listen to them. They have much wisdom that can make your life brighter and richer. When you respect your elders, you set an example for those around you on how to treat older generations.

# Day 12: Truth or Lie?

"OMG, like it was SUCH a disaster at school today," exclaimed Maura as she ran into the kitchen in front of her twin brother, Mark. "Our teacher got so mad and was yelling at all of us!"

Mark raised his eyebrows as Maura unfolded the day for their mom.

"Uh, that's not really what happened," Mark said. "Sure, Mr. Duncan was frustrated because most of the class didn't do well on the test. But he didn't yell at us. He would never do that."

Their mom gazed thoughtfully at Maura.

"Maura...is Mark's version true? Why would you make it sound so bad?"

"I...uh..." Maura scuffed at the kitchen stool with her shoe. "Yeah whatever, I guess how Mark said it is what happened..."

There are lots of verses in the Bible that talk about telling the truth. From Genesis to Revelation, we can see that God desires honesty and integrity in our thoughts, words, and actions.

But did you know that exaggerating the truth, or embellishing the truth, is just another form of lying? In Maura's story, she was right that their teacher wasn't happy with the class, but she made it sound worse than it was. A lot worse. In fact, relaying stories like this can make it seem as if a problem exists where it doesn't.

Sometimes it's hard to not make a story sound more dramatic because we want people to listen to us and to be interested in our stories. Whenever we feel that tug to "fancy up" our stories, that should be a red flag! Because guess what? Once you get started, it's hard to stop. Embellishing stories isn't like turning a faucet on and off. The more you exaggerate, the more easily and often it will happen. Embellishing your stories will become a habit. The more you embellish, the more people will be less likely to trust you.

---

"Teach me knowledge and good judgment,
for I trust your commands."
Psalm 119:66

---

## What about me?

---

Ask God to help you honestly report details of what goes on in your life.

# Day 13: Playing with Fire

I twirled the barrel of my curling iron away from face and…OW! There's nothing quite like burning your finger on the curling iron or flatiron. It HURTS. From stoves to bonfires, to matches and fireworks, fire provides us with heat, cooking abilities, and entertainment. But if you get too close, watch out!

With this knowledge, it would seem pretty silly to scoop hot coals from the campfire or fireplace, hold it against your skin, and not expect to be burned. Of course that will burn you!

Even though we know this would happen with something visible like fire, sometimes we don't realize the same thing happens to us with sin. We think sin won't hurt us or hurt other people, and we push the limits of obedience to see what we can get away with. We try to play with fire.

> "Can a man carry fire next to his chest and his clothes not be burned? Or can one walk on hot coals and his feet not be scorched?"
>
> Proverbs 6:27-28

Maybe you think it won't matter that you cheated on your last science test, or that you lied to your friend, or that you stole money out of your mom's purse. It does matter. We use caution around any type of fire or heat. We need to exercise even more caution with the consequences of sin; turn away from it, run from it, don't try to hold it close. It always burns in the end!

## What about me?

What are some areas that you've tried to "play with fire"? Ask God for help in overcoming temptation in those areas.

# Day 14: Arrows

---

"Like arrows in the hands of a warrior are children born in one's youth. Blessed is the man whose quiver is full of them."

Psalm 127:4–5

---

An arrow? What exactly does that mean for you?

The Bible describes children like arrows in the hands of their parents. Arrows have a specific purpose, right? They are aimed at a target, they are meant to be swift and strong, and they are designed to fly further than the warrior. As children, and definitely as children of God, you are meant to be strong in spirit and move toward the goal which God has set before you. Each generation is meant to builds on itself. Your parents are building on the legacy that was laid out for them, and you will have the same chance. And one day, your kids will build on YOUR legacy...like a long time from now, but you get the picture.

Don't take your role as a child lightly. This is an important training and preparation time so that you can fly fast and straight when the time comes.

## What about me?

Ask the Lord for his help as you train to be one of his "arrows."

# Day 15: Obeying God

Did you know that when you obey your parents (or other authorities) you are obeying God? That should be your real motivation for obeying; not just because they said so, but because when you submit to parents and authorities, you obey God.

> "Children, obey your parents in the Lord, for this is right."
> Ephesians 6:1

Your parents don't give you rules and expectations just because they want to make your life miserable. I know it may feel like that sometimes, but it's not true. They give you expectations and rules to keep you safe and help you mature. They set standards because God has called them to do that. When you obey your parents cheerfully and quickly, you not only bless them, but you honor God with your obedience.

It may be hard to see it or believe it now, but your obedience in the small details is reaping great rewards for you in God's eyes. Your obedience muscles will be that much stronger for when you're grown up and living on your own and don't have your parents checking up on you. Flex those muscles and get good practice now obeying your heavenly father who loves you more than you could imagine.

## What about me?

Ask the Lord for help in building those obedience muscles this week. Remember, you can do all things through Christ who gives you strength! (Philippians 4:13)

# Day 16: Who, Me?

Throughout the Bible, God uses all sorts of people to carry out his will. He uses men and women, old and young. He uses the smart and the powerful. He uses the humble and lowly.

In the book of Judges, we read about a young guy named Gideon. His name was cool, but that's where his cool vibes stopped. Let's just say you probably wouldn't pick him first for the soccer game. Gideon was the "least cool" person in his family who was the least in all of Israel. Yikes! But God used him to defeat an army, an army so big they were compared to the sands on the beach. And there's a lot of sand on a beach.

---

"The Lord turned to him and said, 'Go in the strength you have and save Israel out of Midian's hand.' 'Pardon me, my lord,' Gideon replied, 'but how can I save Israel? My clan is the weakest in Manasseh, and I am the least in my family.' The Lord answered, 'I will be with you, and you will strike down all the Midianites, leaving none alive.'"

Judges 6:14-16

---

Pardon me, Lord? Gideon was confused at first as to why God would even want to use him for mighty adventures. But Gideon stepped out in obedience, and God equipped him and blessed him. He turned him into a warrior, and even later in the book of Judges, he is compared to having the appearance of a prince.

Just like with Gideon, God has a special purpose for all his kids. Don't think just because you don't sit at the cool table at school or because you have braces or a stutter or your clothes are hand-me-down that God doesn't have a place for you. If he could defeat an army with Gideon, imagine what he can do with you!

## What about me?

Pray this with me:

Lord, I don't know all that you have planned for my life, but each day I ask that you give me the courage to follow you and embrace the challenges and adventures you place before me. I trust you with my whole heart! In Jesus' name, amen.

# Day 17: God's House

Have you ever stopped to pick flowers at the park or along the sidewalk? What happened to those flowers after a couple of days? Even if you put them in water, chances are they wilted. Without the proper nutrition, root system, and sunshine, flowers can't keep growing and thriving. The same can be said of us and our involvement in the local church.

As children of God, our church family is like a root system providing the nourishment and strength needed to keep growing in Christ. We learn to build relationships with our spiritual brothers and sisters, supporting each other through tough times and happy times. We are also strengthened by God's presence at church. Worshipping God and listening to his word refreshes us and helps us get ready for the week ahead.

The Church is one of the places we learn about God and how he wants us to live our lives. No matter how old or young you are, God always has a message for you.

If you are removed too long from the church body, or just go every once in a while, you'll be like a flower without a good root system. And just like a real family, the church isn't perfect. The important thing is that we keep listening to God, loving others, and never giving up.

"And let us consider how we may spur one another on toward love and good deeds, not giving up meeting together, as some are in the habit of doing, but encouraging one another—and all the more as you see the Day approaching."
Hebrews 10:24-25

## What about me?

Spend some time thanking the Lord for your church. If you don't get to go regularly, ask the Lord to create opportunities for you to go.

# Day 18: Tough Times

Between ninth grade until my first year in college, my dad lost his job three different times. The job losses were due to different reasons, all beyond our control: the economy or company management, for example. But each time he lost his job, every one of us took the hit hard.

In those years though, God taught me some important lessons.

God showed me that he is the ultimate provider (Philippians 4:19). Yes, parents and other guardians are often the channels through which God provides, but all provision comes from him. He holds unlimited resources and knows exactly what each of his kids needs. I watched God provide for our family before, during, and after those trials, and we never went without.

I also learned that I don't have the power or wisdom to fix every problem, and that's OK. I could tell my parents were hurting, and I wanted to fix that desperately. I wanted to help them. But God is the best comforter, and I had to trust my parents to him.

"Those who know your name trust in you, for you, Lord, have never forsaken those who seek you."
Psalm 9:10

## What about me?

Have you walked through something like this before with your family? How did God comfort or provide for you? How could you comfort a friend who is walking through the same thing?

# Day 19: Same Team

"Carry each other's burdens, and in this way
you will fulfill the law of Christ."
Galatians 6:2

Families can have many different faces, but one thing holds true for all of them: being in a family means you are on the same team. What does that mean? On a regular team, you aren't going to score for the other team on purpose, call your teammates bad names, or switch jerseys mid-game. No! You would never do that.

Let's get even more practical. Think about the last big argument you had with your siblings or parents. Would you have said the same words and insults to your friends' faces? I'm guessing probably not. Why do we treat those who don't live in our houses with more kindness than those who share the same roof? Why is that so hard?

My parents set a standard for my brother and me that the same level of good behavior we used at church, school, or the grocery store should be used at home. It's tempting to get lazy with our actions and words when we're with family. We feel more comfortable, but sometimes that comfort morphs into carelessness. However, you should still use kind words at home and not use them all up away from the house. We should always make an extra effort to be kind to those we are closest to. To the best of your ability, your aim should be to support, love, and "carry each other's burdens" when you can. Because you all are playing for the same team.

## What about me?

How can you show your family that you are on the same team this week? Jot your thoughts down in the space below.

# Day 20: Columns Fit for a Palace

---

"Then our sons in their youth will be like well-nurtured plants, and our daughters will be like pillars carved to adorn a palace."

Psalm 144:12

---

I love these words from Psalm 144. As daughters in training to be leaders in your family, in the community, and in the kingdom of God, this Psalm speaks to our importance in the family structure.

"Our daughters like carved pillars, cut for the structure of a palace."

Daughters can provide meaningful emotional and spiritual support to their families and close friends. As you grow and learn in the Lord, you learn how to use your emotional sensitivities for good and not for drama.

When you feel a wave of drama rising up, look instead for opportunities to listen, to use empathy to put yourself in other's shoes, and to provide encouragement to those who need it. That takes the focus off you and places it on others, giving you some time to collect your thoughts. Don't discount those opportunities by thinking this season of your life doesn't really matter. You have an important role to play now right now as a daughter, as a granddaughter, as a sister.

Your story doesn't start when you are in highs school, when you go to college, or when you move out of your parents' home. You are living your story now.

## What about me?

Has God been giving you opportunities to practice this very same thing? How can you show support to your family, rather than tearing it down?

# Day 21: Columns Fit for a Palace, Part 2

---

"Then our sons in their youth will be like
well-nurtured plants, and our daughters will
be like pillars carved to adorn a palace."
Psalm 144:12

---

Today we are going to continue in the passage that we looked at yesterday. I love this passage because it gives great purpose to your growing up years. The years I lived at home gave me wonderful opportunities to practice listening. My brother loved to talk with me in the evenings, sharing whatever was on his heart. He didn't really need my advice; he just wanted a listening, supportive ear.

My husband today benefits from my listening ear and my advice. By investing in that relationship with my brother, we grew stronger together, but it also prepared me for supporting my husband and cultivating an understanding heart.

I also loved to encourage my dad through notes left around the house and through prayers, something I do for my husband today. The small things you do for your family today do have an impact on tomorrow. Be encouraged that it is not a waste of time. Rather, those things are very worthwhile.

## What about me?

How can you help to serve your family? Do you like writing notes or drawing pictures? What about cooking or watching your younger siblings? Make a list and keep it hand so you're ready to serve your family.

# Day 22: Clothes in a Drawer

When I was a kid, my parents asked me to clean my room, as other parents often do. I was nearing the end of the chore and decided I didn't want to put away my last item of clothing, a pair of pajama pants. Apparently, it would be too much effort to put them away nicely, so I stuffed them in a drawer without folding them.

My bedroom was at the end of the hall, and my dresser was positioned so that anybody could see it from the hallway. As I was stuffing the pants in the drawer, my dad appeared out of nowhere in the hallway and said (partly joking), "Beware, your sins will find you out."

I gasped inwardly. How did he know what I was doing?

While this seems like a meaningless story, it has stuck with me all these years. As we strengthen our obedience muscles (which takes practice), we have to remind ourselves that even if no one else knows about those little sins, God knows. How does that change the decisions we make every day?

The words my dad spoke are from the Bible. They can be found in Numbers 32:

> "But if you fail to do this, you will be sinning against the Lord and you may be sure that your sin will find you out."
> Numbers 32:23

Let's strengthen our obedience muscles by choosing to do the right thing, even when no one is looking. Because we know it's not true that "no one" is looking. God is always looking!

## What about me?

# Day 23: Not Your Fault

God designed marriages to last until death, but because we live in a fallen world, sometimes marriages end before that. The process is hurtful for everyone, especially for kids. One day, your family is in one piece, under one roof. Then, all of a sudden, it's not.

If your family is walking through a divorce, I want to tell you one thing: it's not your fault. It's painful, yes, but it's not your fault.

Grownups make decisions sometimes that as kids, it can be hard to understand. When that happens, God will wrap his arms around you and comfort you. I would encourage you to pray for some specific things during this struggle:

*Pray that God comforts you and helps you through this time.*

*Pray for both your parents, as they need God's love and direction. They are hurting more than you realize.*

*Pray that God sends you good friends to comfort you and help you as your family changes.*

---

"From the ends of the earth I call to you, I call as my heart grows faint; lead me to the rock that is higher than I."

Psalm 62:2

---

# What about me?

# Day 24: Poop in a Candy Wrapper

Think about your favorite candy. My favorite chocolate candy is dark chocolate and my favorite non-chocolate candy would have to be gummy bears or Starburst!

Now, imagine you got your favorite candy for your birthday or Easter, and you opened the wrapper and found...poop.

That's right...POOP. Ew!

That's not real candy! Even though the wrapper looked enticing and wonderful, inside was ugly and awful. A lot of times sin looks like that; enticing and wonderful, but inside, it's ugly and awful. It's like poop in a candy wrapper.

> "And no wonder, for even Satan disguises himself as an angel of light. So, it should not surprise us when his servants also disguise themselves as servants of righteousness."
> 2 Corinthians 11:14-15

Satan knows how to make himself look appealing. That's why we have to stick close to God, daily talk to him, and study his word. This helps us to grow in our discernment, correctly identifying good from evil. Don't fall for poop in a candy wrapper. Sin is still sin, even with pretty packaging.

## What about me?

What are sins that look enticing to you? Tell the Lord which ones are a struggle and ask for his help in overcoming them.

# Day 25: I Know Better

As a kid, I loved the feeling of knowing the right answer and got into a bad habit of correcting those around me when they misspoke, even if it was a tiny mistake. While it's great to know the answers, constantly correcting others is prideful. My parents pointed out that that was called being "wise in my own eyes." What does that mean?

"Wise in your own eyes" comes from the words of Proverbs 3.

---

"Do not be wise in your own eyes; fear the Lord and shun evil. This will bring health to your body and nourishment to your bones."

Proverbs 3:7-8

---

Being wise in your own eyes is dangerous because it ignores the wisdom of those who have more experience and are looking out for your best interest. King Saul in the Bible had a major problem with this. After he was anointed the first king of Israel, he was impatient, took matters into his own hands, and didn't trust God's timing.

He didn't wait for the prophet Samuel to sacrifice to God. Instead, he chose to go to a witch for wisdom (yikes). Later, he wasted time and energy pursuing David for personal reasons. Ultimately, Saul wrote the end of his own story when he took his own life. Over and over, he chose to walk in the wisdom of Saul, and it was his downfall.

## What about me?

How often do we walk in the wisdom of self? I know it's still a struggle for me. So how do you choose differently? Choose humility and fear the Lord, just as the scriptures says. Humility and a listening heart are the cure for being wise in your own eyes.

# Day 26: Not a Burden

Does it feel like your parents and teachers just enjoy making your life "miserable"? That they just WANT to steal your fun?

Parents, teachers, and other authorities in your life carry a great responsibility to mold and shape you, and sometimes that means making tough decisions for your benefit. It may be hard to believe, but trust me.

In the meantime, sighs, eye rolls, shoulder slumps, and whiney voices sometimes escape you. Though they may not show it, those little signals of exasperation and frustration wear on your parents and teachers. Let's not make their job any harder than it already is. Here's what the Bible has to say about that:

---

"Have confidence in your leaders and submit to their authority, because they keep watch over you as those who must give an account. Do this so that their work will be a joy, not a burden, for that would be of no benefit to you."

Hebrews 13:17

---

Making their job harder doesn't help you at all. It may hurt you, in fact.

*What about me?*

Choose today to help your leaders by trusting them, responding and obeying with a cheerful spirit.

# Day 27: Saying Goodbye

I don't like talking about death, but my hope is that today's devotional provides help for whenever you have to say goodbye to someone or something that you love like a pet, a grandparent, or a friend.

First of all, it's OK to be sad. Everyone shows their sadness in different ways. Crying, talking, silence, even being angry are all of ways of showing grief. This was something I didn't understand when I was your age. Don't be afraid of grief, and don't be afraid of all the different ways people express grief.

Second, if your loved one was a Christian, they are home with Jesus! They are having a party! They are not sick, hurting or confused any longer. While we still miss them on Earth and life won't be exactly the same, we know we will see them again one day.

If your loved one was not a Christian or you weren't sure, don't be anxious. God will draw near and give you extra comfort. Focus on the good times you had with your loved one because no one can take that away from you.

Through it all, God is near and will never cease to comfort you. I promise. He has done it time and again for me when I have lost someone I loved. He is the perfect comforter, understanding our hearts when no one else can.

---

"The Lord is close to the brokenhearted and
saves those who are crushed in spirit."

Psalm 34:18

---

## What about me?

---

If you have recently lost a loved one, these activities can help you work through the sadness:

1. *Learning a new song or scripture about comfort*
2. *Talking with a friend or trusted adult*
3. *Writing or drawing how you feel in a journal*

*Keep those lines of communication open with a* trusted adult because they can provide extra help and guidance. There's no reason to suffer in silence or grieve alone.

# Day 28: Devotion in Motion

---

"Therefore, as God's chosen people, holy and dearly loved, clothe yourselves with compassion, kindness, humility, gentleness and patience."
Colossians 3:12

---

I love the verb in this scripture: clothe. Clothing yourself with qualities like humility and kindness means that every day, you put them on – just like getting dressed in regular clothes! And one of the first places we should clothe ourselves with these qualities is in our own home. So today is one of our Devotions in Motion!

List below some ways you can show kindness to a family member this week and try at least three items on your list. Here are some ideas:

*Help your younger brother or sister with homework or a chore.*

*Write your mom or dad a thank-you note for being an awesome parent.*

*Call a grandparent and tell them hi and ask about their day.*

Now get out there and show some kindness!

# What about me?

Kindness

Mow someones yard

help my brother With homeWork

Wash the dishes

Ask my parent How was they're day

Help my friends With Clarinet

# Day 29: The Story of Ruth

The book of Ruth is a short book in the Bible that tells a beautiful story of kindness. Ruth is a young woman who lost a lot of special people in her life; her father-in-law died, and not long after that, her husband, her two children, and her brother-in-law also died.

She traveled back with her mother-in-law, Naomi, to her hometown of Bethlehem to make a new life. Especially in Biblical times, unmarried women had a difficult time making a living on their own and had to fight hard to provide for themselves.

In Bethlehem, Ruth would leave Naomi every morning to follow the harvesters and pick up the grain they'd missed during the harvest, a common job for the poor during that time. Soon, she met the owner of that field. That owner happened to be a distant relative of Naomi's named Boaz.

Boaz was a kind man who was generous as well as wealthy. He was moved by Ruth and Naomi's heartbreaking tale and instructed the rest of his workers to not bother Ruth. He even told them to leave behind more grain for her. But his kindness doesn't stop there.

Boaz was so moved by Ruth's story and her bold yet wise demeanor that he decided to marry her. And theirs was a royal marriage in the making. Ruth and Boaz were the great-grandparents of King David. And King David was an ancestor to King Jesus.

Boaz's act of kindness and Ruth's willingness to accept it had a ripple effect throughout eternity.

## What about me?

What kind of effect will your kindness have on the people around?

# Part 2:

## Squad Goals

# Getting Started

Besties. BFFs. Besties for the resties. Squad. Homies. Friends.

Whatever you call them, friends fill our lives as we interact with them at school, at church, in the neighborhood, on the soccer team, in the dance room, and beyond. Friends can make life fun, and help us get through the worst of times. On the other hand, sometimes friends are the REASON for the worst of times if they've betrayed or hurt us. What's a girl to do?

God gives us lots of ways to navigate changing and sometimes messy friendships in order to help us bloom. Are you ready? Consider going through this section of the study with a group of your friends. You all can learn and grow stronger in your relationships.

Let's dive in!

# Day 30: Being a Good Friend

From school to church to after-school activities, chances are you're surrounded by friends. Some friends you've known for a long time, others are new relationships. Some friends will end up staying in your life for a long time (I've known my best friend since I was six and we are still friends!) and some will only be your friends for a season. With all this time spent around friends, it's important to learn how to be a good friend and how to look for good friends. What do you look for in a friend? Honesty? Positivity? A good sense of humor? List other qualities that are important to you below.

The qualities I appreciate in a friend are loyalty, positivity, an understanding heart, a relationship with God, and the ability to have fun! We all want to have a little fun!

Now, take a look at your list, and take a look at yourself. Do you possess these qualities, or is there room to improve? In order to have good friends, you also have to be a good friend. The qualities you are looking for in a friend may be qualities people are looking for in you.

---

"Perfume and incense bring joy to the heart,
and the pleasantness of a friend springs from
their heartfelt advice."
Proverbs 27:9

---

## What about me?

Ask God to help you be a good friend as you look for good friends.

# Day 31: Your Squad

Friend: One attached to another by affection or esteem. (Merriam Webster)

In the "What About Me" space, list or draw your own group of friends, your "squad," and spend some time thinking about them. How long have you known them? Did you meet them at church or school? Somewhere else? What do you all like to do together? What's a favorite story or inside joke you share?

The Bible also spends a lot of time talking about friends and those who you choose to spend time with. One of my favorite verses about friends is found toward the end of the book of Proverbs.

---

"As iron sharpens iron, so one person sharpens another."

Proverbs 27:17

---

What does this verse mean? As you and your friends do life together, your character, your choices, your words are forming and shaping them. And their character is doing the same to you. Wow! That's powerful. Let this verse help you as you spend time with friends, meet new pals, and influence those around you. Your words and actions are helping shape each other.

# What about me?

# Day 32: Cliques

Laura shifted in her spot as Mrs. Stevens, the drama teacher, worked with another group of students across the stage. Mrs. Stevens had just worked with Laura and a group of girls on their next scene, but three of the girls kept talking and giggling among themselves. Again. Those three were always in their own little world, and could rarely be bothered with anyone else.

Why are they being so annoying? Don't they realize we just changed the opening lines? Laura wondered.

Jackie, one of the trio, soon realized she didn't know her part.

Serves her right, Laura thought. She had the same chance to learn it as I did and she didn't... she was too caught up with her special little clique.

Laura saw how ugly it looked to not be friendly to everyone. She decided to be genuinely friendly to everyone that she could, and not exclude certain people for random reasons, even when that meant helping Jackie learn the changes to the script.

Have you been in a situation like Laura? I have found in my own life that it usually turns out better to try to be friendly with those around me, even if I can't be friends with everyone. The least I can do is smile, look people in the eye, help where I can, and make people feel included.

# What about me?

> "Do nothing from rivalry or conceit, but in humility count others more significant than yourselves."
> Philippians 2:3

Don't fall into the clique trap. You never know what you're missing out on by only focusing your attention on a small, prideful group of friends. Be humble. Be friendly. Say no to cliques!

# Day 33: Two Wrongs

When I was a kid and my brother wronged me in some way, I was tempted to get back at him. And I know when I wronged him, he wanted to get back at me, too. My dad would usually remind us that two wrongs don't make a right.

It's a saying that's been around for a while, but what does it mean? It means that when someone else does something wrong, it doesn't help for you to also do something wrong in order to fight back. In fact, retaliation often makes the situation worse, gets you into trouble, and goes against God's plan for us.

> "Do not repay anyone evil for evil. Be careful to do what is right in the eyes of everyone... Do not be overcome by evil, but overcome evil with good."
> Romans 12:17, 21

You would expect to feel better after you retaliated or got revenge. But you won't. It's a trap. Fight back with good instead, whether that means speaking up for someone, keeping your mouth shut, helping a person in need, or telling the truth.

In your friendships, in fact, in all your relationships, don't fight back with evil. Choose to overcome evil with good.

## What about me?

Have you ever wanted to get revenge on someone? Have you ever gone through with it? How did it ultimately make you feel? Ask God for wisdom to follow through on the wisdom from the verses above when it comes to dealing with friends who have wronged you.

# Day 34: Friends Who Are Boys

I remember for a long time, I thought boys were icky. Very icky. They were loud, rude, and weird. I wanted to be as far away from boys as I could. I mean, sure I noticed if they were cute, but that did not override the gross boy factor.

But as it happens for every girl, at some point, you don't want the boys to go away. You wouldn't mind if they hung around and talked. You wouldn't mind if they noticed you, even if it makes you giddy and nervous all at the same time.

What's a girl to do?

It's OK to just be friends with boys. Listen to them and hang out with them if you want, all while practicing discretion and kindness.

There is often a lot of pressure, especially at school and even church, to "like" a certain guy and have him "like" you back. It's not worth your time to obsess over that. Focus on being friends. It will be much more fun, I promise.

---

"She is clothed with strength and dignity; she can laugh at the days to come."
Proverbs 31:25

---

# What about me?

If you are clothed in God's strength and dignity, you can be free to be friends with who he calls you to be friends and not worry about which guy likes or doesn't like you. You can laugh at the days to come, dear daughter of the king.

# Day 35: Finding Good Friends

Good friends…

Good friends are loyal and stick by your side, even when the "cool crowd" makes fun of you, even when it would be easy to join the other side.

Good friends don't abandon one friend for another.

Good friends listen and are interested in your life and don't just blab on about their own interests and activities.

Good friends follow through on what they say, even if it means making sacrifices. They don't ditch you if "better" plans come up.

Good friends don't talk behind your back, in person or on social media.

Good friends aren't perfect, but they are the perfect people to be imperfect with!

---

"A friend loves at all times."

Proverbs 17:17

---

## What about me?

Pray this with me:

Lord, I thank you that you gave us the perfect example of a friend in Jesus. Help us to love and serve others like he did. In Jesus' name, amen.

# Day 36: Peer Pressure

"C'mon, everyone's doing it!" "You're not going to be lame, are you?" "I knew it! You are such a drag!"

Have you heard lines like these, or have you said similar ones? These words fall into the category of peer pressure. Peer pressure is trying to force someone to make a choice for the sake of fitting into the crowd. This type of pressure doesn't give people the space to make the right decisions for themselves, and it can quickly turn dangerous. Let's see what God's word says about peer pressure.

"Do not be misled: Bad company corrupts good character."
1 Corinthians 15:33

These scriptures say hanging out with bad friends ruins your reputation (even if you have a good one!) and that the world's pattern isn't the one we should be following.

"Do not conform to the pattern of this world, but be transformed by the renewing of your mind. Then you will be able to test and approve what God's will is—his good, pleasing and perfect will."
Romans 12:2

As children of God, we are called to be different. Those who try to fit in and give in to peer pressure find themselves doing or saying things they know aren't right. In order to fit in with the crowd, these people disobey God. Often times, it's impossible to please both people and God. If we constantly try to fit in and give in to peer pressure, we can't follow God's commands at the same time. We can't do both, so we must choose.

God created something beautiful when he created you—something unique and wonderful that had never existed before in the history of the world. Don't sell out to be a copy of someone else. Be who God created you to be and follow his commands. You never know: your courage to say no to peer pressure may give someone else the courage to say no, too.

## What about me?

# Day 37: Jesus Conversations

What do you and your friends like to talk about? Nail polish? Your next ballgame or performance? Boys? Hairstyles? That one hilarious Instagram video? As girls, we often cover a wide range of topics when we are chatting with our friends. I know I do when I'm talking with my Mom or friends!

But I have another question for you: how often do you talk about Jesus with your friends?

If Jesus is our constant companion, if he is supposed to be our best friend, it would seem like he would come up in conversation a little more often than he does.

> "But as for me, it is good to be near God. I have made the Sovereign Lord my refuge; I will tell of all your deeds."
> Psalm 73:28

We usually talk about what is most important and most exciting to us. Jesus should be our most important and exciting thing, all the time.

# What about me?

Here are some good ways to bring up Jesus in a conversation with friends who are believers:
- What scripture has meant a lot to you lately?
- What are some things you are praying about?
- What is Jesus doing in your life?

And some questions for friends who don't know Jesus:
- Can I be praying about something for you?
- What's on your heart right now?
- Would you like to visit church with me sometime?

Who knows, those conversations might lead to them wanting to know more about Christ!

## Day 38: Friends Are Not Your Everything

You know how it goes. Life is going great, and then one of your friends tells you that another one of your friends said THIS about you, and now everyone at school is talking about it. You are crushed and don't know how you could ever be friends with that friend again. Or maybe you and your group of friends used to do everything together, and then someone picks up a new after-school activity with another group of friends and your squad drifts apart.

While it's not fun to be in a fight with your friends or to go through changes in your relationships, it's a good reminder that your friends are not the most important thing in your life. It may be hard to believe, but it's true.

As a child of God, he is the most important thing. He is the one who defines you and gives you worth. We are designed to love him with all our hearts.

If you base how you feel on the mood of your friends, your mood will be out of your control. One moment you'll feel great; the next moment you'll feel awful. And that cycle will repeat every week!

Enjoy your friends, but remember, they are not your everything. God is your everything, and he can supply your every need.

> "Love the Lord your God with all your heart and with all your soul and with all your strength."
> Deuteronomy 6:5

# What about me?

# Day 39: Satisfied

What would it take to satisfy you? I mean really make you happy? A new phone or outfit? Attention? More followers on Instagram? More compliments? We seek all sorts of words, possessions, and experiences to fill us up and make us feel happy. The truth is, worldly things will never satisfy us in the end. They will never complete us. In fact, they can make us feel even more empty than when we started if we aren't careful.

---

"For he satisfies the thirsty and fills the hungry with good things."
Psalm 107:9

---

Only God truly satisfies. Only God truly fills us up. It's not to say we can't enjoy kind words from friends, a new outfit, and exciting trips. But God must fill us first. Instead of demanding that other people pay attention to us, we need to turn our attention to him. In doing so, we are satisfied and freed up to enjoy the blessings God has placed in our lives.

# What about me?

Think about your day and ask yourself, "Am I focusing my attention on God or trying to get attention for myself?" On a sticky note, draw an arrow pointing up and place the note where you will see it throughout the day. This will remind you where your attention needs to be, and also remind you that only God truly satisfies you.

# Day 40: Forgiveness

All friends fight. It's going to happen. You talk it out and forgive each other. Then what? It's hard to forget sometimes, especially if they hurt you. Then the next time you all fight, out spills all the past hurts, and everyone's upset.

> "Love prospers when a fault is forgiven, but dwelling on it separates close friends."
> Proverbs 17:9 (NLT)

Dwelling on a matter can separate even the closest of friends. If your friend (or you) has asked for forgiveness, and the past has been put right, you are not acting in love to continually bring it up. 1 Corinthians 13 also says that "love keeps no record of wrongs."

It's not that you completely forget, but whenever the situation comes to mind, say a quick prayer like, "Thank you, Jesus, for your forgiveness toward me. I have forgiven _____ for _____, and I'm not changing my mind." The more you do this, the less the situation will come to mind. When you do this, you can build a stronger friendship.

## What about me?

Is there something that you need to forgive a friend for? Is there something you need to ask a friend to forgive you for? Write out your words here as practice, then pray and ask God for help to make things right with your friend. Understand that it may take time, but we can always trust the results with him.

# Day 41: Gossip Girl

We all know her. You know...that girl. The girl who loves to talk loud and long about other people. And sometimes what she has to say isn't nice.

She's a gossip girl.

Gossip Girl isn't a nice title, especially for girls who are God's children. Gossip tears others down and stunts your growth on your way to blooming in God's garden. The Bible mentions gossip by name several times, and God's message is clear: AVOID GOSSIP.

---

"A perverse person stirs up conflict, and a gossip separates close friends."

Proverbs 16:28

"A gossip betrays a confidence; so avoid anyone who talks too much."

Proverbs 20:19

---

Unless you know something about a friend that could be dangerous to herself or others (in which case you need to tell a trusted adult), don't spread hurtful words about people behind their backs. Be kind to those you don't know well and treat everyone how you want to be treated. For your friends who you know well, let your words be seasoned with truth and love.

Don't drag people's private lives out into the open and play guessing games with them. Avoid gossip and spread truth and love!

## What about me?

Is gossip a temptation for you? Are there friends you need to apologize to for words you have spread about them? How can you set an example of avoiding gossip in the future? Sometimes that may look like changing the subject or even leaving the room if gossip heats up.

# Day 42: Dwell on What is Right

---

"Finally, brothers and sisters, whatever is true,
whatever is noble, whatever is right, whatever is
pure, whatever is lovely, whatever is admirable—
if anything is excellent or praiseworthy—think
about such things."
Philippians 4:8

---

This is one of my favorite verses. Whenever fearful and anxious thoughts try to come into my mind, I hold up this checklist to see if they can stay. If they don't pass this checklist, the thought does not get to stay in my mind!

By filling my mind with thoughts that do meet this checklist, my mind is filled with peace.

Are my thoughts?

- ✓ True
- ✓ Noble
- ✓ Right
- ✓ Pure
- ✓ Lovely
- ✓ Admirable
- ✓ Excellent
- ✓ Praiseworthy

## What about me?

Is it time to do a thought check-up? Kick out thoughts that fall short of this list and focus on the ones that line up with this scripture.

# Day 43: Imitate God

Have you ever tried to act like someone else, or imitated them? Maybe your favorite movie character or TV personality? How about someone in your family or a friend of yours?

What are you doing when you imitate someone? You are acting and talking like them, and maybe even thinking like them Did you know that God calls us to imitate him, or in other words, live our lives like him?

> "Imitate God, therefore, in everything you do, because you are his dear children."
> Ephesians 5:1 (NLT)

God desires for us to imitate him because we represent him here on earth. But what does that look? When you imitate God, that looks like loving others and thinking of others first. It means following his will, not your own. It means that you choose true and kind words.

Every day you are exposed to footage and photos of singers, actors, comedians, and influencers that will let you down in the long run if you try to imitate them. God will never let you down. He is the perfect role model!

## What about me?

How else would you imitate God? Jot down your thoughts below.

# Day 44: Jesus' Squad

As we've already seen, the Bible has a lot to say about friends. In fact, friends and friendship are mentioned more than 100 times throughout the Old and New Testaments! As you learn more about friendship in the pages of God's word, we know that Jesus is always a good example to look at. Throughout his life on earth, we see him extending love and truth to all he met, but he was close friends with a small group of twelve, the disciples! Even within the group of disciples, there were three men who were closest to Jesus: Peter, James, and John.

Peter was one of the first disciples Jesus called to himself. Jesus entrusted the care of his mother to John as he was on the cross, and James was with him in the Garden of Gethsemane, where Jesus spent his last hours before his arrest and ultimate crucifixion.

These guys weren't perfect (far from it at times), but Jesus allowed them into his life at his most vulnerable times, because even Jesus needed the support of his friends, his "squad." They gave Jesus the support he needed, and because of Jesus' investment in them, they went on to do amazing work for the kingdom of God.

---

"I no longer call you servants, because a servant does not know his master's business. Instead, I have called you friends, for everything that I learned from my Father I have made known to you."

John 15:15

---

*What about me?*

How does it feel to be called a friend of God? What can you learn from Peter, James, and John when it comes to being friends?

# Day 45: Words that Pack a Punch

We've talked a lot in these pages about the importance and power of the words you speak. But what about the words you write?

There are more ways than ever to write something and share it with a large group of people. Texting and social media make it too easy to turn private thoughts into public discussion.

This is not always a good thing. Whether its words you write in your journal, messages to your friends, or thoughts you post online, those words tend to spread further than you think. And if the words you've shared aren't good, the damage can be widespread.

Untrue and hurtful words shared online can ruin people's reputations (how others view them) and even get them into trouble.

As children of God, we must have a higher standard! Getting a laugh or a like isn't enough reason to share something that is mean and hurtful. Choose kindness, and if you still struggle with what you post, flip the situation around. How would you feel if someone was sharing mean words about you?

The words you write are just as important as the words you speak. More importantly, written words stick around a lot longer than spoken words do, and they spread a lot farther.

"Whoever derides [speaks harshly about] their
neighbor has no sense, but the one who has
understanding holds their tongue."
Proverbs 11:12
*(Clarification mine)*

What about me?

# Day 46: Stand by Your Friends

The other table erupted in laughter, paused as the kids eyed Emma and Paige's table, and then dissolved into laughter again. Paige stared down at her lunch, eyes filling with tears. One by one, the other kids surrounding the girls picked up their trays and moved to join other groups. Soon it was just Emma and Paige.

"Just go. Everyone else left. I'm sure you don't want to eat at my table. I can't do my own homework, remember?" Paige spit out the words through the tears that overflowed.

Emma moved closer and patted Paige on the shoulder.

"You're my friend. Even if you have trouble with your schoolwork and need help, that doesn't change who you are. I'll still be your friend. I like you whether you can do your homework or not."

Sometimes our friends go through hard times or struggles. That's when they need our friendship the most. Maybe they have learning challenges or family problems and other kids make fun of them because they're different. As children of God, we should set the example of remaining a good friend even when it's rough, even if you may get made fun of, just by being their friend.

## What about me?

Do you stick by your friends only in the good times, or do you stay in the bad times, too?

---

"One who has unreliable friends soon comes to ruin, but there is a friend who sticks closer than a brother."
Proverbs 18:24

---

# Day 47: Pig Jewelry

As young ladies in the Lord, we must learn to not put jewelry on a pig. Wait, what?!

---

"Like a gold ring in a pig's snout is a beautiful woman who shows no discretion."

Proverbs 11:22

---

The Bible tells us that a young lady without discretion is like jewelry on a pig. Jewelry on a pig is out of place and foolish, right?

According to the Merriam-Webster dictionary, discretion is "the quality of being careful about what you do and say so that people will not be embarrassed or offended."

A young lady who shares every single thought and detail of her life with everyone around her is out of place and not attractive.

For instance, you might talk about bathing suits with your friends who are girls, but it wouldn't be discreet to talk about that subject in front of boys. Or maybe your parents are going through a rough patch in their marriage, or one of them is sick. They may want you to practice discretion and not share all the details with your friends

It takes practice to build those discretion muscles, and it can be hard to know what's appropriate to say and what's not. But if you pray and ask the Lord for help, he will show you what to do.

*What about me?*

Place a picture of a pig where you'll see it regularly as a funny reminder of the importance of practicing discretion.

# Day 48: Be a Peacemaker

Have you noticed that some friends always seem to have drama swirling around them? And then some friends don't? Which group would you fall into? Truthfully, we've all been in both camps at one point or another.

As daughters of the king, we are called to be peacemakers. Not troublemakers who stir up drama, not even peacekeepers who may try to sweep real problems under the rug instead of dealing with them. Peacemakers demonstrate how to have inward peace with the Lord and cultivate a spirit of peace among their squad.

---

"Blessed are the peacemakers, for they will be called children of God."

Matthew 5:9

---

If we constantly stir up drama, it muddies the water, and it makes it harder to stand out as God's kids. Stirring up trouble and drama to look cool or interesting is not an activity or a hobby. It's a sin. Choose to be a peacemaker, not a peace stealer. Make friends with peace and break up with drama, "so that you may become blameless and pure, "children of God without fault in a warped and crooked generation." Then you will shine among them like stars in the sky." (Philippians 2:15)

# What about me?

# Day 49: Contagious

Do you know what it's like being around a joyful person? They are always smiling, have lots of energy, and can always make you feel good about yourself.

Maybe you are that person in your family or your group of friends, or maybe not. But remember, smiles are contagious! It's hard to stay mad or gloomy around smiling people. Joy is meant to be contagious.

---

"Your love has given me great joy and encouragement, because you, brother, have refreshed the hearts of the Lord's people."
Philemon 1:7

---

You never know what someone is going through. Maybe by smiling at others, saying hi, or just talking to them, they may be encouraged and refreshed. And who knows – maybe because they have been refreshed by you, they will go on to encourage the next person they come across. Spread joy!

## What about me?

Are you someone that refreshes the hearts of those around you? You can start today simply by smiling or sharing a kind word with those you meet.

# Day 50: Everybody's Doing It

Like any other kid, I argued with my parents from time to time. But one argument I was sure to lose every time was, "But everyone else is doing it!"

That was the surest way to NOT get what I wanted, and it would probably guarantee some punishment to follow. My parents were wise and reasonable parents, and they knew better than to fall for that line.

Everybody else is doing it? That's a horrible reason to jump on board. As you learn to walk with God, you learn to follow God's word and listen to the Holy Spirit, instead of mindlessly getting swept up with the crowd.

Stop and think: should I be doing this? Why am I doing this? Would this make Jesus happy? Would this make my parents happy?

If you have doubts on any of these questions, you shouldn't be doing the deed in the first place. If you have to make excuses in your mind about something, that's also a red flag. Let God and wise authorities be your guide in life, not peer pressure.

---

"Walk with the wise and become wise, for a companion of fools suffers harm."

Proverbs 13:20

---

## What about me?

# Day 51: Monster Mouth

We chew with it. We blow bubbles. We wear braces. We speak with it. We sing and play instruments with it. But for all our mouth does for us, it's one of the hardest things to control.

That's right, the mouth is one of the wildest, messiest creatures we will ever try to tame. God spends a lot of time instructing and even warning us on the ways of our tongue.

As the old saying goes, we were given two ears and one mouth for a reason. We should do more listening than talking! Too much talking can get us into trouble, from literally talking when we shouldn't to saying something that deeply hurts another person.

---

"Sin is not ended by multiplying words, but the prudent hold their tongues."

Proverbs 10:19

---

To let your mouth blab on without thinking of others and without enough listening is to invite sin to your party. If you are prudent (wise and thoughtful), you won't be afraid of shutting your mouth from time to time.

As girls, it's easy to get carried away with our mouths. One minute, we're talking about something innocent like shoes or hairstyles, then the next thing we know we are bad-mouthing someone's outfit, not realizing they've slipped into the room and heard everything. Yikes. Attack of the monster mouth. Let's tame the monster and close our mouths.

## What about me?

Ask the Lord to help you control your mouth in a way that honors him.

# Day 52: Surrounded by God

When I was in college, I experienced for the first time the loss of a friend who was my age. Early one rainy morning, she was killed in a car accident. After that happened, I felt scared and unprotected in a way that had never felt before.

In the days that followed, God encouraged me with many scriptures that spoke to him surrounding his children. I needed those promises. I needed to be reminded that God does take care of his kids.

When bad stuff happens, it's never because God caused it or wished it upon his kids. We live in a fallen world, and mistakes, tragedies, and injustices are going to happen. God said that himself (John 16:33). But what we are promised is that no matter what does happen, God is right there with us. And he never abandons his children.

I still struggle with fear from time to time. I still struggle because it was hard to lose that friend (even though I know I'll see her again someday in heaven). But I call to mind scriptures like the one that follows, and I am encouraged.

> "The salvation of the righteous comes from the
> Lord; he is their stronghold in time of trouble.
> The Lord helps them and delivers them; he
> delivers them from the wicked and saves them,
> because they take refuge in him."
> Psalm 37:39-40

# What about me?

You can look up the word "help," "deliver," or, "saves" in the back part of your Bible called the concordance. The concordance will list all the scriptures that have to do with a certain topic. Write down some verses like the one above that you can look back at whenever you go through a troubling time.

# Day 53: Pursue Peace

Did you know that peace does not automatically download into our lives? Peace does not just appear in your life without any effort.

Certain scriptures help us see that connection by using "pursue" and "peace" in the same sentence. Peace is something you have to seek, something you work toward. If you are pursuing a goal, you are doing everything you can to reach that goal.

---

"Let us therefore make every effort to do what leads to peace and to mutual edification."

Romans 14:19

"...seek peace and pursue it."

Psalm 34:14

---

Seek peace and pursue it. Do you say you want peace, but continue to gossip and spread rumors? That's not pursuing peace. Do you stir up fights and arguments? That's not pursuing peace. As children of God, our actions and words should line up, so let's make sure with both, we are pursuing peace.

## What about me?

What are ways you can pursue peace with your family? With your friends? Ask God for help in pursuing peace in your life.

# Day 54: Desert Island Survival

If you could only bring three items with you on a desert island, what would they be? Take some time to list them below.

It's so hard to pick, right? Food, items to build a shelter or hold water, knives or sticks for building things...the list could go on! But you know what? A ton of followers on Instagram or the perfect Insta filter probably wouldn't help you much on an island far at sea.

But we definitely act like our social networks are necessary for our survival in real life. How much time do you spend primping for the perfect selfie? How much do you crave that little notification bubble lighting up?

Social media has not always existed, believe it or not. People made plans, formed friendships, and took pictures without social media. While these things are fun, you can't let them define you. You can't let them fill you where God should be filling you.

You are beautiful and you are smart and you are thoughtful: you don't need a notification bubble to tell you that. God has already decided you are worth dying for because he sent his son to die on a cross for you.

---

"See what great love the Father has lavished on us, that we should be called children of God! And that is what we are!"
1 John 3:1

---

I can't think of a better notification to receive!

# What about me?

# Day 55: Starting Over

Jordan rubbed her sleeve under her nose for the tenth time this morning as she looked at her childhood home. The last time. The last time she would see this special house. Her dad heaved the moving van door shut and fished some keys out of his pocket.

"All right gang, let's load up. Time to get on the road."

Jordan's dad had gotten a new job, one that the family needed, but it was across the country in California. They had to leave their church, their school, and all their friends and family.

Nothing would ever be the same again. All of Jordan's friends… She couldn't help asking herself, why do we have to move so far away?

Have you ever faced a move like Jordan? Starting over in a new town is hard, and you may be worried about the challenges you'll face. Maybe you're afraid you won't be able to make new friends. Or maybe you're afraid your new friends won't be as good as the ones you're leaving behind. Maybe you're dreading going to a new youth group and being the awkward loner. Maybe instead of getting your own room in the new house, you have to share with your sister.

Whatever you're facing, know that God is with you! He didn't stay behind in your old town; he is right there with you, and he knows what it feels like to be uprooted. Jesus was constantly moving around from city to city and staying with different people. He didn't have a house he went home to every night.

"Never will I leave you; never will I forsake you."
Hebrews 13:5

This is God's promise to us! He won't leave us to fend for ourselves.

## What about me?

If you are about to move or make a big transition, pray that God helps you in your new town or in this new chapter of life. Pray for awesome new friends and a place to plug in at church. He is able to meet those needs! If you have a friend that is facing a big move, you can pray these same things for her.

# Day 56: Devotion in Motion

We've covered so much in this section about building healthy friendships, and now I want to place a challenge before you. While it's nice to text or comment compliments on our friends' pictures, I want to challenge you for the next week to give your compliments in person as well, or maybe even write them a note. There's just something special about hearing a compliment from your best friend, or re-reading a sweet note!

Don't just think those compliments, open your mouth and speak them!

---

"Therefore encourage one another and build each other up, just as in fact you are doing."

1 Thessalonians 5:11

---

# What about me?

# Part 3:
## Growing Stronger

# Getting Started

What's your favorite fruit? For me, it would have to be strawberries and peaches! In this last section, you are going to about a different kind of fruit – not fruit that grows on trees or on a vine, but Fruits of the Spirit.

> "But the fruit of the Spirit is love, joy, peace, forbearance, kindness, goodness, faithfulness, gentleness and self-control. Against such things there is no law."
> Galatians 5:22-23

Along with these strange fruits, you are also going to learn about growing in all sorts of circumstances you face, whether they are trials or triumphs.

Grab a snack of your favorite fruit, and let's get started!

# Day 57: What's That Fruit For?

"But the fruit of the Spirit is love, joy, peace, forbearance, kindness, goodness, faithfulness, gentleness and self-control. Against such things there is no law."
Galatians 5:22-23

This passage is known as the fruits of the Spirit. While reading about these strange fruits, I wondered who gets to enjoy this fruit? Is it just for you to enjoy? Or are other people blessed by your fruit? Why or why not? Jot down your thoughts below.

I believe one of the reasons God wants us to grow the fruit of the Spirit in our lives is because our fruit is a big way we can show love to others.

"Jesus replied: 'Love the Lord your God with all your heart and with all your soul and with all your mind.' This is the first and greatest commandment. And the second is like it: 'Love your neighbor as yourself.'"
Matthew 22:37-40

By planting and growing the fruit of the Spirit in your life, you meet both of these commands. You are loving the Lord with all you are, and you are loving others as yourself. If you choose peace over worry and love over hate, you are loving the Lord with your whole self. When you choose kindness over meanness and faithfulness over untrustworthiness, you are treating others how you would want to be treated.

That's why the fruits of the Spirit are so important. By growing them in your garden, they bless others and help you follow all of God's commands.

## What about me?

Write out the fruits of the Spirit on a sticky note or index card and put it near the fridge to remind you of the fruit God is growing in you.

# Day 58: Building Muscle

In sports, gymnastics, dance, or cheer, you repeat different exercises to build strong muscles so that you can perform harder and more complex skills. Sometimes those exercises aren't fun, but they are necessary to progress in your sport or activity.

Building spiritual muscle is no different. Right now, through small challenges, struggles, and disappointments, you are building the strength for skills you'll need down the road. The difficulties you're facing may not be fun right now (and that's OK), but you'll be glad for them later.

---

"Consider it pure joy, my brothers and sisters, whenever you face trials of many kinds, because you know that the testing of your faith produces perseverance. Let perseverance finish its work so that you may be mature and complete, not lacking anything."

James 1:2–4

---

It can be easy to get discouraged if you're going through tough times. But it may help to look at your struggles as exercises and conditioning for greater moments down the road. And just like with physical conditioning, the more you work a set of muscles, the easier it gets to use them. And the more you trust God with the struggles in your life, the easier it will be to trust him with bigger needs.

# What about me?

# Day 59: Words That Build

Our words have the power to build up or tear down. It amazes me that our words have the power to construct beauty in us and around us, but they also have the power to demolish and destroy.

It takes a certain fruit of the Spirit (self-control) to measure our words as they come from our brain and out our mouths. We have to ask ourselves, "Is what I'm about to say going to build or tear down?"

> "Do not let any unwholesome talk come out of your mouths, but only what is helpful for building others up according to their needs, that it may benefit those who listen."
>
> Ephesians 4:29

The Bible also says the enemy is one who comes "to steal, kill and destroy." (John 10:10) As children of God, our words should do the opposite! Our words should give life, build up, and strengthen.

So exercise your self-control muscles to guard your words. Because just like toothpaste out of a tube that you can't put back, words spoken can't be taken back.

## What about me?

Have you been building up with your words? Why or why not? When do you find it the hardest to speak kind words? Pray and ask God to help you in those moments to speak kind words.

# Day 60: Easier Than You Think

Do you ever wonder if God hides himself from you? Sometimes it may feel like he has hidden his commands inside of riddles, like it's a guessing game we're bound to lose. That's just not true.

---

"But the word is very near you. It is in your mouth and in your heart, so that you can do it."

Deuteronomy 30:14

---

This verse promises us that following God's word is not beyond your abilities; in fact, it's in your mouth and heart! I don't know about you, but I need to be reminded of that every day because sometimes making the right choice is so hard. You don't want to be happy for your friend who won the award you wanted. You don't want to walk your dog. You don't want to confess to cheating on the test. Do any of these situations sound familiar?

These are hard choices to make. But through Christ's power and his word that is "very near," you can choose to make the right choice and have self-control (control over your emotions and feelings) and follow after God. He gives you the strength and the ability to do just that!

## What about me?

Write out today's verse on an index card or sticky note and put it somewhere where you'll see it regularly. The next time you find yourself having a hard time obeying God, remember the verse above. The ability to do the right thing is easier and closer than you realize!

# Day 61: Led with Love

Do you ever feel like all God wants to do is spoil your fun? It sure can feel that way. Sometimes we can think God is like a policeman or a judge who is always mad at people and always eager to punish, but that is simply not true! While God does discipline his children, it's always done in love. There is a beautiful scripture in the book of Hosea that shows God's heart toward his wayward children.

Hosea is in the middle of the Old Testament and is written by another of God's prophets, Hosea. (Yes, the book is named after the author. Pretty cool!)

> "I led them with cords of kindness, with bands of love."
> Hosea 11:4

God leads us, he directs us, and yes at times has to discipline us, but he does it in love and kindness. He's not an angry judge or policeman, but a loving father who wants the best for his kids. I am so grateful for that!

## What about me?

Pray this with me:

Heavenly Father, thank you for your faithful love that leads me, guides me, and surrounds me. I don't have to worry about "hoarding" your love, for you have plenty to give to all your children. Because you have plenty, I have plenty. I know you have my best interest at heart. Help me to continue to trust you! In Jesus' name, amen.

# Day 62: Honesty

Do you think you could ever trick God? The Bible is full of stories of people who thought they could trick and lie to God, but it never ended well for them.

Before we can practice honesty with those around us, we first must be honest with ourselves, and honest with God. You can't trick God. You can't lie to him. Sometimes being honest hurts, or is scary, but those are temporary feelings. Feelings of freedom and peace will last much longer than fear if you choose the truth over lies.

The enemy wants us to believe the hurt and fear will last a long time, but that's the trick. The enemy himself can't even tell the truth. So why do we waste time believing him? As God's children, we must choose honesty, even if it will hurt for a little bit.

---

"Truthful lips endure forever, but a lying tongue lasts only a moment."

Proverbs 12:9

---

## What about me?

Is there something in your heart that you haven't been honest about with God? I encourage you to lay out everything before God and let him work with his truth and mercy. We can trust our hearts with him who made us and loved us first.

## Day 63: Be Bold in Who God Made You

Are you a shy person or a loud person? Or are you a mixture of both? It's entirely possible to be a mixture of both!

As we talk about the fruits of the Spirit like kindness and gentleness, I want you to realize there is not just one way to show these fruits. You don't have to be quiet and timid to show kindness. You can be bold and loud and still be gentle. You can be tender while still being confident and bubbly.

Everyone's personality is different, and those differences make us so wonderfully special! God made you uniquely you when he created you with all your style and sparkle. The world may tell you that sarcasm is queen and sass is how you get your way. But be encouraged to be your own special brand of kindness. Be your own bubbly form of gentleness. Be bold in who God created you to be.

---

"We have different gifts, according to the grace given to each of us."

Romans 12:6

---

## What about me?

Of all the fruits of the Spirit, which ones seem to come most naturally to you? Which ones seem more difficult? Thank the Lord for the ones that come a little easier (we still need to work on those!) and ask him for help for those that are more difficult.

# Day 64: Beyond Our Understanding

---

"And the peace of God, which transcends all understanding, will guard your hearts and your minds in Christ Jesus."
Philippians 4:7

---

This is one of my absolute favorite scriptures. The promise is so powerful!

Storms are going to come through our lives: maybe your parents will separate, your best friend will move, or you'll struggle in school. It doesn't mean you've done something wrong. Trials are a part of life.

But in the midst of these storms, God's peace is available to us in vast quantities. His peace will never run out! I don't know about you, but that's encouraging to me.

Even when we don't understand how we could have peace in a situation, God is there to provide it. That's what the phrase "transcends all understanding" means. We aren't going to understand the peace he gives us fully because it's so hugely wonderful, but that peace is there to stay. We can depend on it.

## What about me?

Pray this with me:

Heavenly father, I praise you for how wonderful your peace is. Thank you for how it guards my life. I choose to trust you no matter the circumstances. In Jesus' name, amen.

# Day 65: Corrie Ten Boom

Have you ever heard of Corrie Ten Boom? Corrie and her family helped to hide and transport many Jews during World War II nearly eighty years ago. They helped to save the lives of countless families.

Eventually, the Nazis did capture Corrie and her family and take them away to a concentration camp.

Corrie and her sister Betsie were in the same camp, but they were separated from the rest of their family for a long time. While in the camp, Corrie and her sister endured hunger, sickness, and unspeakable living conditions. The prisoners weren't usually allowed to have personal belongings, but Corrie managed to get a copy of the New Testament from one of the nurses.

Reading the Bible sustained her and gave her peace while she was in the concentration camp. She was able to be strong for her sister and for those around her.

A prison camp is perhaps the last place you'd expect to find peace. But as Corrie and the other ladies gathered to read God's word, they found hope and peace in plenty.

"But now in Christ Jesus you who once were far away have been brought near by the blood of Christ. For He himself is our peace..."
Ephesians 2:14

# What about me?

# Day 66: Diamonds

I am fascinated with the process required to produce diamonds. Diamonds start out as inconsequential lumps of carbon deep within the earth and through dynamic forces and extreme pressure, a brilliant gem is formed. What was once hidden, unlovely material deep in the earth is turned into a valuable stone, one of the hardest substances in the world.

The connections between diamonds and our spiritual development are too big to miss. We start out as rough, unlovely material and then God with loving, yet firm hands shapes us using the Holy Spirit, trials, and the pressures of this life.

We are transformed into people of substance, people of value, people that are made to withstand the scratches life leaves on us.

Diamonds have been highly valued in cultures across the world for millenniums, but I wonder if sometimes ignore the fact that diamonds did not start out as diamonds. You don't get to enjoy the brilliance, the shine without the heat, the pressure, and the trials.

If you are feeling the heat and the pressure have been turned up in your corner of the world, take heart. You are undergoing the same process required to form a diamond.

"Consider it pure joy, my brothers and sisters, whenever you face trials of many kinds, because you know that the testing of your faith produces perseverance. Let perseverance finish its work so that you may be mature and complete, not lacking anything."
James 1:2-4

What about me?

# Day 67: The City

Sometimes we see in the movies a town that has been destroyed by an army, or robots, or aliens, or a natural disaster. The line of defense is compromised, the people are unprotected, and soon the city is in chaos. The Bible says we are like that city if we don't operate with self-control. What does that mean?

> "Like a city whose walls are broken through is a person who lacks self-control."
> Proverbs 25:28

Without self-control, our line of defense would be damaged, we would be unprotected, and our lives would be in chaos. Practicing self-control lends order to our lives and keeps us safe and protected.

Also, by practicing self-control, you not only take care of yourself, but you protect those around you. A city doesn't just have one person living in it. No, there are many people that live in the city. Many people suffer when the walls are broken down. Practice self-control to keep your city safe.

## What about me?

What are some ways that you can practice self-control? Jot them down below!

# Day 68: Mary and Martha

"OK, the rolls will be done in five minutes. Peter, can you come cut the meat? What can I get everyone to drink? Oh! We haven't even set the table! Mary? Mary? Girl, where are you?"

Martha stood in the doorway to the living room with arms crossed and stared at her sister. Mary the dreamer. Mary the oblivious. Mary, who managed to be absent when real work needed to be done.

Jesus spoke to the few gathered in the front room, his gentle words soothing all who could hear, including Mary, who sat on the floor near him.

"Mary!" Martha hissed again.

Heads swiveled in her direction.

"Jesus, can you please tell my sister she is needed in the kitchen?"

---

"Martha, Martha," the Lord answered, "you are worried and upset about many things, but few things are needed—or indeed only one. Mary has chosen what is better, and it will not be taken away from her."

Luke 11:41-42

---

I've always been fascinated by this story. To be able to sit at the feet of Jesus and drink in his words, his peace? Incredible. But I sympathize with Martha as well. She was seeking peace in being perfect, in making sure everything was just so when True Peace was sitting right in her living room. She just needed to go sit at his feet.

## What about me?

Are you seeking peace in the wrong places? Do you need to spend some time sitting at Jesus' feet this week?

# Day 69: Do Not Be Afraid

All four gospel writers share the story of Jesus walking on water.

A storm whipped up on the sea when the disciples were on the boat, and Jesus walked out to them on water. Because that would obviously be freaky to see, Jesus' first words to them were, "Do not be afraid. It's me."

I love this about the story. The disciples were scared and worried they would drown. They didn't find peace in their equipment. They didn't find peace in each other. They didn't find peace in their own skills.

Their peace was ultimately found in knowing who Jesus was. At this point, the disciples had already spent a lot of time with Jesus. They'd seen him perform miracles and preach incredible messages. They knew who Jesus was, and that was why they trusted him in that moment, trusted that everything was going to be OK

The same is true for us. The more time that we spend talking to God and listening to him in prayer, reading our Bibles, and serving Him, the more we see what he is capable of. Then, the next time a storm whips around our boat, we'll be able to hear Jesus calling through the storm, saying, "Do not be afraid, it's me."

"As they sailed, he fell asleep. A squall came down on the lake, so that the boat was being swamped, and they were in great danger. The disciples went and woke him, saying, 'Master, Master, we're going to drown!' He got up and rebuked the wind and the raging waters; the storm subsided, and all was calm. 'Where is your faith?' he asked his disciples. In fear and amazement they asked one another, 'Who is this? He commands even the winds and the water, and they obey him.'"
Luke 8:23-25

## What about me?

# Day 70: Press Pause

At many points in the Bible, God guides his people do certain things along with him to accomplish a victory in a battle or overcome hardship. From singing, to holding up Moses's hands, to striking a rock with a stick, God never had his people take a step of faith in the same way.

On the other hand, many times we see God asking his people to be still, to hold their ground, to wait. God sometimes chooses to act alone.

---

"The Lord will fight for you; you need only to be still."

Exodus 14:14

---

Sometimes, God wants to grow our faith by choosing to hit the pause button and let God act. Sitting and waiting can sometimes be the hardest choice, because it feels good to be doing something, anything. It feels good to be in control, but that's the very lesson God may be teaching you: he's in control, and we're not. We need to walk in his peace, and trust that he is God and will fight for us. Let's practice pushing the pause button and letting God do his thing.

## What about me?

Draw a picture of a watch or a clock below to remind you that God's timing is the best timing!

# Day 71: A Quiet Soul

Growing up, I was a little bit nosy. OK, maybe more than a little bit. I always wanted to know who my mom was talking to on the phone and all the details about her friends. I guess I thought adult friends were more interesting than what I had going on. I wanted older-people knowledge because I thought it would make me feel more grown-up, more sophisticated.

God speaks to this attitude in Psalm 131.

"My heart is not proud, Lord, my eyes are not haughty; I do not concern myself with great matters or things too wonderful for me. But I have calmed and quieted myself, I am like a weaned child with its mother; like a weaned child I am content."

Psalm 131:1-2

There are a lot of good truths in this verse. It first speaks to knowing your place and having peace about it. For young girls who are growing into teens, this can be a hard lesson. But King David is the one who wrote this Psalm, so if even a king had to be reminded of his place before God, then so do we.

The next verse talks about calming yourself. The imagery behind this verse speaks of having peace, even if you don't get everything you want. You know you can be quiet and calm, even when you don't get every question answered or every little whim met. That's part of growing up, physically and spiritually.

## What about me?

The next time you find yourself in a restless, nosy mood, read this Psalm again. If you let yourself get quiet, God's peace will cover your heart and soul.

# Day 72: Rainbows and Clover

One day, two pictures came up in my Facebook feed. The top picture was a painting by a Christian friend of mine. The painting depicted a lone tree in a serene field with a rainbow arching across the top of the page. It radiated God's love and peace. This scripture was below it:

> "For he will rescue you from every trap and protect you from deadly disease. He will cover you with His feathers. He will shelter you with His wings. His faithful promises are your armor and protection."
>
> Psalm 91:3-4

Directly underneath was a photograph by another friend of mine, not a Christian. She had found a four-leaf clover on vacation and her caption read:

"I found a four-leaf clover...maybe I will finally have some good luck!"

These pictures present such different worldviews. I happen to know that at that time, the non-Christian friend could have used everything I was seeing in the rainbow picture in her life.

She knew of God, but she did not know him personally. The other girl could walk in peace throughout her life because of the promises she'd found in scripture. Her life, as well as the lives of all who walk with God, has those promises as its foundation, its covering, its front and rear guard. I don't know about you, but knowing God is my protection makes me feel good.

With all that we experience in life, we don't want to be left holding a measly four-leaf clover, or any symbol of luck that the world manufactures. We want the assurance of the One who made those four-leaf clovers...and the rainbows.

## What about me?

Think back to the two girls with their pictures. Which one describes you?

Have you trusted God as your savior, and are you resting under his protection? Or are you just wishing on clovers and good deeds to get you through the day? If you'd like to nail that down for sure, let's take care of that right now! You can know for sure that God is the Lord of your life. If that's a decision you want to make, feel free to pray the prayer below in your own words. Then, tell a caring Christian adult about your decision. They'll help you with the next steps.

Pray this with me:

*God, I don't want to depend on clovers and good luck to get through the day. I need you as my savior, to guide my whole life. I want to know you personally. I believe you came and died for my sins and rose again so I could have a personal relationship with you. Thank you. I want to be your kid and rest in your protection. Help me to follow you every day. I love you. Thank you for loving me. In Jesus' name, amen.*

# Day 73: Of Snow and Flowers

I love being outside (especially when the weather is nice). I love going for walks or hikes, or even just reading a book on our porch on a sunny afternoon. God meets me there in the sunshine and soft breezes, and I'm delighted by his peace.

What else in nature demonstrates peace? Clouds drifting by on a summer's day? Butterflies flitting from flower to flower? A baby deer with its momma? Snow falling on a silent winter afternoon?

At the time of writing this first draft, I'm watching snow fall gently outside my window. Peaceful is the word that comes to mind. It's like God is decorating a cake with powdered sugar!

God's peace is evident throughout nature. Sure, he demonstrates his power through volcanoes, thunderstorms, and the crashing waves of an ocean! But he has also tucked away hidden messages of his peace throughout the world. You just have to look for them.

The Lord gives strength to his people; the Lord blesses his people with peace.

Psalm 29:11

## What about me?

If the weather (and your parents) allows it, take your quiet time outside today and in the space below, journal or draw different things you experience in nature that demonstrate peace. It could be a bird on a branch, a cat resting in the sunshine, a breeze that touches your cheek, or the scent of trees or rain. Whatever touches your heart, thank the Lord for the many ways he showers his peace on his children.

# Day 74: A Future for You

Like storm clouds gathering on the horizon, perhaps chaos is gathering around you right now. Maybe fighting and arguing are erupting in your home, your school, or your community because of sin and evil choices. Recent tragedies may have shocked you or those you love, tragedies and events caused by those bent on evil.

> "Do not fret because of those who are evil or be envious of those who do wrong; Consider the blameless, observe the upright; a future awaits those who seek peace."
>
> Psalm 37:1, 37

God encourages us to not worry when evil happens, and he reminds us there is a future for those who seek peace. If you allow yourself to get swept up in the evil around you, the future looks bleak. So seek peace. Don't fret over evil. Our God is still the Great I Am, no matter what happens. Nothing can knock him off the throne.

## What about me?

Pray this with me:

Heavenly Father, even when evil and chaos is swirling around me, I trust your heart, and I ask for your peace to cover me like the warmest blanket. I depend on you! In Jesus' name, amen.

# Day 75: Shhhhh

"The Lord said, 'Go out and stand on the mountain in the presence of the Lord, for the Lord is about to pass by.' Then a great and powerful wind tore the mountains apart and shattered the rocks before the Lord, but the Lord was not in the wind. After the wind there was an earthquake, but the Lord was not in the earthquake. After the earthquake came a fire, but the Lord was not in the fire. And after the fire came a gentle whisper. When Elijah heard it, he pulled his cloak over his face and went out and stood at the mouth of the cave."

1 Kings 19:11-13

If we imagine God talking, we might think he would show himself in an earthquake or mighty wind. That makes sense, right? He is the Almighty God, after all.

But in this passage, he reveals himself in a whisper. Quiet. Calm. Yet still powerful. Loud enough for Elijah to hear, but different enough for him to know it was indeed the Lord.

Quieting our hearts so we can hear God's still small voice takes practice. It takes practice to tune in to his voice. But good changes happen when we let peace rule our hearts and choose to listen to that gentle whisper.

## What about me?

Find a quiet corner in your room or outside and get still before the Lord. Read today's verse again and underline the words or phrases that stood out to you. If something is standing out to you, that is often the Lord's way of speaking to you! Write it down and ask him how to apply it in your life.

# Day 76: The Armor of God

Did you know that you have been given armor? Crazy, I know! God equips each of his children to fight the enemy, but the armor may not look like a regular helmet or bulletproof vest. Each piece of spiritual armor has a purpose!

**Belt of truth**: like a belt holds up and gives structure to clothing, truth holds everything up and gives it structure. Without it, weakness strikes, and lies become easier to believe.

**Bulletproof vest of righteousness**: God's righteousness covers our heart and no attack can snatch us out of God's hand.

**Shoes of peace**: When you have the proper shoes on, you can take run, jump, do whatever you need to do. Since Jesus told us to go into the entire world to preach the gospel, these shoes make us ready to run, jump, or walk to spread God's word of peace across the ocean or across the street.

**Shield of faith**: Our faith cripples the enemy. We must pick up our shield when he sends bullets and arrows into our camp. They fall away in the presence of faith.

**Helmet of salvation**: Our mind is the battlefield. Salvation is the perfect protection!

**Sword of the Spirit**: The word of God is our only offensive weapon, the only weapon we can attack with. It cuts the enemy to pieces and forges a path for us. Don't leave your sword at home!

If you were to just use or put on one piece of armor, it wouldn't do you much good. You have to use all of it, every day! Your armor is only good if it's actually on your body and in your hand.

# What about me?

Read Ephesians 6:10-18, the armor of God passage. Jot down any thoughts that come to you, or questions you have about the pieces of armor. Ask God for help in knowing how to use each piece of armor.

# Day 77: Listen

Do we know how to listen to God? I mean, really listen. Sadly, I think about how often I fill the time I spend with God with words...so many words. Not all bad ones. But do I stop enough to listen to him? Do I pause long enough to hear his voice?

---

"Know this, my beloved brothers; let every person be quick to hear..."

James 1:19a

---

In any relationship, there is talking and listening; giving and taking. Why should communication with God be any different?

Our society puts a lot of emphasis on words. We learn early to fill the silence with words. They don't even have to be helpful or true, it seems. We can't let that thinking bleed into our relationship with Jesus. If you find yourself lacking in the area of listening, don't hesitate to relax in God's presence, close your eyes, and just listen. Whether he has something to say to you or simply wants to bless you with his nearness, let him have the floor.

God always refreshes me when I take time to do this. I have felt his arms wrap around my soul. He is eager to do the same for you.

# What about me?

For today's quiet time, find a quiet place and listen for God's voice. You can open with prayer, but don't feel like you have to pray the whole time. At the end of your quiet time, jot down anything you think the Lord was saying to you.

# Day 78: Springtime

Spring is without a doubt my favorite season. I love to soak up the sunshine and watch all the trees and grass as they green up. I love to see all the flowers start to bloom.

All the freshness and newness are so welcome after a long, dark winter.

All through the winter, the plants, trees, and grass prepare to bloom again, even though we can't see them at work. They are working behind the scenes to burst forth with new growth and beauty.

Sometimes God works the same way in our lives. We can't always see what he is doing—sometimes it feels like nothing is going on! Do you ever feel like that?

The Bible promises that we can trust that God knows best, and we can rest and be patient that he is working in our lives.

---

"For I know the plans I have for you, declares the Lord. Plans to prosper you and not to harm you, plans to give you a hope and a future."

Jeremiah 29:11

---

## What about me?

Just like flowers waiting to bloom in the gentle spring sunshine, God's plans for our future are waiting to spring up and put out beautiful blooms in the garden of your life. So, don't give up!

# Day 79: Abraham's Impatience

In the book of Genesis, God makes a special promise to one of his children, Abraham. Abraham and his wife were elderly, but sadly, they didn't have any kids of their own…yet.

God made a promise to Abraham and his wife Sarah that they would have a child, even though they were much older than most parents. God was going to build the nation of Israel through this couple. Excitement filled their hearts.

And so they waited…and waited…and waited for the baby that God had promised.

After years of waiting, they grew impatient and took matters into their own hands—never a good thing. What they did caused a lot of pain and confusion. (You can read more in Genesis 15-17, 21) God visited them again and reassured them they would indeed have a child of their own.

And then finally, baby Isaac came along. Abraham was 100 years old, and it had been more than fifteen years since God had made that first promise to him.

Did God forget? Was God procrastinating? Of course not! God's schedule is not always our schedule, and if he has promised something, we can trust him to do it.

As we work on the fruit of patience, we must remember to trust God's timing and not take matters into our own hands. He is worthy of our trust.

"By faith Abraham, when called to go to a place he would later receive as his inheritance, obeyed and went, even though he did not know where he was going. And by faith even Sarah, who was past childbearing age, was enabled to bear children because she considered him faithful who had made the promise. And so from this one man, and he as good as dead, came descendants as numerous as the stars in the sky and as countless as the sand on the seashore."

Hebrews 11:8, 11-12

## What about me?

What are you waiting on right now? How can you show that you are trusting God's timing?

# Day 80: Can't Wait to Be King

David was a young kid, not much older than you, when God gave him a special promise. God told him he had been chosen as king over Israel! David, the youngest in his family whose after-school job was taking care of sheep. Pretty ordinary. Very un-fancy.

But he didn't get to be king the next day, the next month, or even the next year. It was several years before that became true. In the years between when God made the promise and when God brought it about, lots of things happened. There were lots of events, lots of trials, and lots of important victories.

God was preparing David for the job of being king.

As a shepherd, David had to protect his father's sheep. He watched over them, rescued them if one became lost, and fought off predators like bears and lions.

Later on, David fought a giant soldier (literally, a giant) and many armies. And he was prepared for those battles because he'd practiced on bears and lions.

Before he was king, David served the first king of Israel, Saul. While David was good friends with Saul's son, Jonathan, Saul was mean to David. Saul was jealous of David, gave him difficult jobs to do, and even tried to kill him. But David remained faithful and patient, waiting for his time to come.

Sometimes, it's hard to wait for something exciting. We want what we want now! But God is faithful to prepare us for the road ahead. David wasn't perfect, but God used him in amazing ways. We have to be patient with God's timing.

# What about me?

# Day 81: Necessary Ingredient

Cookies without sugar would taste awful. Cakes without baking soda would be flat and hard. Lemonade without lemons just wouldn't be the same. Mashed potatoes without milk or butter wouldn't be creamy and smooth.

In cooking and baking, there are usually a few ingredients you can fudge on if you don't have them. But then there are those ingredients that without them, you shouldn't make the dish. They are too important to leave out.

Patience is one of those necessary ingredients in our walk with the Lord. Without patience, our faith grows much more slowly, and we don't see the fulfillment of God's promises as clearly.

It's like sugar in cookies or lemons in lemonade. You just have to have it.

---

"We do not want you to become lazy, but to imitate those who through faith and patience inherit what has been promised."
Hebrews 6:12

---

Patience isn't the ingredient we can skip or exchange. Let's practice putting patience into the mixture of our day, every day!

## What about me?

Ask your parents or guardians if you can mix up some lemonade or cookies. As you prepare your tasty treat, ask the Lord for strength to be patient.

# Day 82: On Being Content

Think about something you want right now. Something big. Like something you think you won't ever be happy until you have. Maybe it's a new bike, or maybe you've been begging your parents for a new puppy. Maybe you have to have that new phone because everyone has that new phone. Now imagine you did have those items you think you have to have.

What would be your next "have to have"? A new tablet? Another dog? That expensive pair of jeans? Even though you got what you already said you wanted, doesn't that end up creating more want?

Can you see that this pattern could continue? Getting a new phone or bike would not slack your desires. Your desires would only change. If we don't learn to set our watches to God's time, we will continually feel disappointed and unfulfilled.

I don't believe that the Lord wants his kids to live in a constant state of unhappiness and impatience, of waiting for that next exciting thing or even just waiting for the next thing.

I believe we must practice not seeing each stage of life as somehow incomplete, but as a whole chapter that contains exactly what God wants it to. And as book chapters build on one another, so do our life chapters.

---

"Give thanks in all circumstances for this is the will of God in Christ Jesus for you."

1 Thessalonians 5:18

---

## What about me?

Believe that God has placed in this day exactly what he wants you to have in it. Practice being patient and content, versus constantly sending God your wish list.

# Day 83: Resist Pride

---

"You said in your heart, 'I will ascend to the heavens; I will raise my throne above the stars of God...I will make myself like the Most High.'"
Isaiah 14:13-14

---

These verses send shivers up my spine, and not the good kind. These verses refer to the fall of Satan. He thought he could elevate himself to the same level as God, and that prideful attitude was his downfall. Have you dealt with the feelings that led you to believe that you are better than other people? Or maybe those thoughts even tempted you to think you knew better than God. Pride is powerful and sneaky, and it is much stronger than we realize.

We are God's children, but not equal to God. When we forget that, pride makes our hearts hard and unusable. The Bible says God "opposes the proud, but gives grace to the humble." (1 Peter 5:5) As you continue to learn more, remember that God is the one who gives knowledge, but that knowledge is not to be used to put others down or elevate ourselves. It's to grow in our own skills and abilities to be used for the kingdom. Ultimately, it's used to bring him glory.

## What about me?

What are some areas you're tempted to be prideful in? Ask the Lord for help to stay humble.

# Day 84: Servant King

In almost any story you read, kings and rulers have lots of people serving them. Servants do all the dirty work, and the kings appear to have all the fun; they eat the best food, have their fancy clothes brought to them, and go hunting on horses that have been saddled for them. They seem to have all their chores done for them. Kings never have to lift a finger.

Jesus set a different example for a king. He didn't expect others to serve him, he served others. He was humble. He had the mindset of a servant in that he didn't have any trouble putting the needs of others first.

> "Just as the Son of Man did not come to be served, but to serve, and to give his life as a ransom for many."
> Matthew 20:28

Jesus didn't come to lounge in his backyard with a servant fanning him as he drank lemonade and ate chicken nuggets. Jesus came to love people through actively, humbly serving them.

# What about me?

Heart check time: do you expect to be served, or do you seek to serve others where you can? Let's follow Jesus' humble example and find ways that we can serve those around us.

# Day 85: Growing Through Tough Times

My second year of high school was a hard year for me: in school, in dance, and in my walk with Christ. I was truly stretched and challenged and at the end of it, I wrote down some thoughts. I'm sharing them here, just for you!

It felt like I had moved up a level in a video game, but all of my tricks and moves from the last level didn't work in the new level. That year was about letting God show me how to survive in the next level. It wasn't always fun. But it is what the Lord wants. He wants me to continually learn, not become stagnant in my life. After many new and unexpected challenges had been placed in my path, I realized that managing them was a part of the growing process. It just took me a long time to figure that out!

But I guess the Lord decided I was ready to step it up. He began to teach me about myself and about himself in ways I had never thought of before. I learned to go to the Lord first, not to my emotions. He never failed to bring me a word of encouragement or instruction, just when I needed it. Even today, I am learning to see challenges in a new way—in a good way. Everyone is going to have them, but meeting challenges and overcoming them is what separates God's children from the rest of the world.

## What about me?

Challenges are what mold you and me into victorious children of God, so don't be surprised when they come your way.

---

"I have told you these things, so that in me you may have peace. In this world you will have trouble. But take heart! I have overcome the world."
John 16:33

---

# Day 86: Patient with Ourselves

Sometimes the hardest person to be patient with is ourselves. We want to be perfect, we want to be the best, and we want it yesterday.

Does this sound like you? Then I have good news for you.

It's OK to not be perfect. It's OK to not have it all together. No one expects you to be perfect. So, take a deep breath... and let it out. You aren't perfect, but life isn't going to end because of it.

---

"Not that I have already obtained all this, or have already arrived at my goal, but I press on to take hold of that for which Christ Jesus took hold of me... I press on toward the goal to win the prize for which God has called me heavenward in Christ Jesus."

Philippians 3:12, 14

---

## What about me?

The important thing is to keep moving forward. Leave perfection for when we spend eternity with Jesus. Embrace this beautiful adventure of life on earth. Be patient with yourself.

# Day 87: Keep Following Me

*I walk beside my God*
*Down the road of life;*
*Sometimes seeing, sometimes not-*
*Sometimes happy, sometimes not-*
*Still He whispers in my ear,*
*"Keep following me."*

*Some friends I'd traveled with*
*On the road of life*
*Suddenly dart ahead or fall behind.*
*I long to help the one or*
*Chase the other.*
*So He whispers in my ear,*
*"Don't follow them. Keep following me."*

*When storms threaten to batter me*
*On that road, I just want to sit and cry,*
*Yet when balmy breezes kiss my face,*
*It's easy to forget from where I have come.*
*Then I hear that familiar whisper,*
*"Keep following me."*

*And though friends have fallen behind*
*Or moved ahead and clouds ever lurk above the road,*
*My Lord takes my hand and whispers,*
*"Keep following me," and I whisper back,*
*"I will follow you."*

"To this you were called, because Christ suffered for you, leaving you an example, that you should follow in his steps."
1 Peter 2:21

"When he has brought out all his own, he goes on ahead of them, and his sheep follow him because they know his voice."
John 10:4

# Day 88: Trusting When You Can't See

Today we are going to hear from my friend Marissa on trusting God even when you don't see how your situation can get better.

*I walked through one of the most difficult times in my life when I was 15 years old. I had experienced the first death in my family as my grandpa passed away suddenly. My family didn't see how the pain could get any worse until just one week later, I had to be hospitalized for anemia, which is a bleeding disorder due to low iron that was causing me to bleed to death.  My family was incredibly scared to hear the doctors say they had never seen a case like mine so severe and were afraid they may not be able to help me.*

*My parents prayed diligently for God to provide the doctors with answers, and after two days, the bleeding stopped and my iron levels were back to normal.  I received six blood transfusions during my stay in the hospital and while going through all the treatments, it was difficult to keep a positive mindset, but with mine and my family's faith in God, we had the strength to face each day.  Although I was in critical condition I remember quoting Jeremiah 29:11 as I awaited the doctor's treatments.*

---

"For I know the plans I have for you' declares the LORD, 'plans to prosper you and not to harm you, plans to give you hope and a future."
Jeremiah 29:11

---

*This verse provided me the comfort I needed for this experience in a way that nothing else could. I knew that I might die, but I became OK with it because I knew that my previous decision to follow Christ and be baptized gave me the pathway to heaven, and if God was ready for me to come home to Him, then so was I.*

*I put my trust in God's promise to keep me from harm and to prosper in my future, and with that, I was able to overcome my sickness and see my life as a gift from God with a purpose to fulfill. When you put your faith in his plan for your life, there is nothing to fear, not even death.*

## What about me?

# Day 89: How Does Your Fruit Grow?

Your circumstances are changing all the time. Each year is a new grade with new teachers and new friends. Sometimes you move to different towns, or your parents get new jobs. Sometimes you change churches. Sometimes everything is going great. Sometimes life isn't so easy.

The beautiful thing about the fruit of the Spirit is that it is not dependent on circumstances. We can keep growing in joy, love, and peace no matter whether times are looking up or looking down.

In fact, our fruit probably grows even better in tough circumstances!

When it's hard to be happy, let God teach you how to find joy.

When it's hard to be patient, let God work in his timing.

When it's hard to love someone, let God love through you.

You'll be amazed at the fruit he can grow!

"...by their fruit you will recognize them."
Matthew 7:20

## What about me?

As you look back over this study, what character qualities have you grown in? What areas do you struggle with?

# Day 90: Joy in Being God's Girl

As we finish our time together in Bloom Book 2, I want you to be encouraged and know that it's a joy to be a girl, especially God's girl. The world may send different messages about what it's like to be a girl, but remember that you are the finishing touch in God's creation. God created Eve last, and then he was done creating the world and everything in it. How cool is that?

> "Many women do noble things, but you surpass them all. Charm is deceptive, and beauty is fleeting; but a woman who fears the Lord is to be praised."
> Proverbs 31:29-30

God created you with a big heart: a heart to love others, a heart overflowing with joy, a heart ready to take on whatever is next. God created you to reflect his heart, his beauty.

God created you to be a girl, and he has good plans for you. The world needs strong, beautiful young ladies who love God deeply and are confident in their identity in Christ. The world needs young ladies who are courageously blooming in their friendships and relationships with family.

Those are the girls who change the world.
Rejoice in being God's girl!

*What about me?*

# You Did It!

You did it, my friend! I'm so proud of you that you finished this book. It's OK if you missed some days here and there. (You can always go back and finish them later!) The point is you grew closer to God and are more equipped to build strong relationships with your friends and family.

Relationships are not always easy. Loving those in our life is messy work because sometimes the people who frustrate us the most are the ones we are closest to. But the relationships are always worth it. You just have to keep growing, keep forgiving, keep loving.

We have the perfect example of a loving brother, a loyal friend in the person of Jesus Christ. When we lose our way, we can look to him for guidance and understanding.

Thank you for going along with me on this journey, and I'll talk to you again in Bloom Book 3, where we'll learn what God has to say about our role in the church and our community. I can't wait!

Love,
Samantha

# A Note of Thanks

This book, like any book, would not be possible without the input, expertise, and support from a lot of people.

To Kurtis, thank you for believing in me (and among many things), acting as my IT and layout department, accountant, and showing me how to dream and cast a vision for the future. I love you.

To my editor Robin and my designer Emily. Thank you for making Book 2 come to life!

And to many others for your wise input and critiques along the way.

Coming 2019:

# Bloom Book 3

# About the Author

SAMANTHA HANNI is the author of Change the Conversation and the Bloom devotional series. Her work has also appeared on Devotional Diva, To Love Honor and Vacuum, Families Alive and in the OCHEC Informer. From teaching dance classes to leading Sunday school and small groups, Samantha has taught and mentored students since 2007.

She graduated with a degree in journalism, and her passion is encouraging other people and seeing God's truth make a difference in their lives.

Samantha and her husband Kurtis live in Oklahoma City with their dog, Podrick.

# How to Connect with Samantha

**Website:** mrshanni.com
**Instagram:** @samanthahanni
**YouTube:** Samantha Hanni
**Facebook:** @samanthahanniauthor

12727602R00117

Made in the USA
San Bernardino, CA
11 December 2018